Newton was pulled off the production line at "FURRY FELLOWS TOY FACTORY" by quality control for having two odd eyes and lop-sided ears. He also failed to meet the Furry Fellows Guaranteed Minimum Stuffing Requirement as laid down in old Mr Fellows original mission statement. He was saved from a fate worse than death by old Mr Fellows himself who took a shine to our little chap and took him home with him (he was quite lonely). Newton's Law of life (not be confused with Sir Isaac Newton's law of gravity, although that's pretty good too), is simple;

"Try hard enough, don't give up and things will turn out right in the end".

This may be considered a little naive by some, who put it down to watching too many movies. Newton's laconic wit is derived from his own life experience (and from watching too many movies). Newton became known for his many sayings or quotes about life, which collectively is "Newton's Law".

Newton is not a "hearts and flowers" bear...he would rather be holding a double chocolate chip cookie (wouldn't you?)

Newton's Law

Friends and Family Organiser

This book belongs to

Kathleen Beecroft

Address

Telephone

Xmas 2020

Nature and Co.
'Decorators to the World'

Name

Address

Telephone

Mobile

E-mail

Name

Address

Telephone

Mobile

E-mail

Name

Address

Telephone

Mobile

E-mail

Name

Address

Telephone

Mobile

E-mail

Name

Address

Telephone

Mobile

E-mail

Name

Address

Telephone

Mobile

E-mail

Name

Address

Telephone

Mobile

E-mail

Name

Address

Telephone

Mobile

E-mail

Name

Address

Telephone

Mobile

E-mail

Name

Address

Telephone

Mobile

E-mail

Name

Address

Telephone

Mobile

E-mail

Name

Address

Telephone

Mobile

E-mail

Name

Address

Telephone

Mobile

E-mail

Name

Address

Telephone

Mobile

E-mail

Name

Address

Telephone

Mobile

E-mail

Name

Address

Telephone

Mobile

E-mail

need a hug...

Name	Name
Address	Address
Telephone	Telephone
Mobile	Mobile
E-mail	E-mail
Name	Name
Address	Address
Telephone	Telephone
Mobile	Mobile
E-mail	E-mail
Name	Name
Address	Address
Telephone	Telephone
Mobile	Mobile
E-mail	E-mail

Name	Name
Address	Address
Telephone	Telephone
Mobile	Mobile
E-mail	E-mail

Name	Name
Address	Address
Telephone	Telephone
Mobile	Mobile
E-mail	E-mail

	Name
	Address
	Telephone
	Mobile
	E-mail

Name	Name
Address	Address
Telephone	Telephone
Mobile	Mobile
E-mail	E-mail
Name	Name
Address	Address
Telephone	Telephone
Mobile	Mobile
E-mail	E-mail

Name

Address

Telephone

Mobile

E-mail

clear your mind –
make a list...

Name

Address

Telephone

Mobile

E-mail

Name

Address

Telephone

Mobile

E-mail

Name

Address

Telephone

Mobile

E-mail

Name

Address

Telephone

Mobile

E-mail

Name

Address

Telephone

Mobile

E-mail

Name

Address

Telephone

Mobile

E-mail

Name

Address

Telephone

Mobile

E-mail

Name

Address

Telephone

Mobile

E-mail

Name

Address

Telephone

Mobile

E-mail

Name

Address

Telephone

Mobile

E-mail

Name

Address

Telephone

Mobile

E-mail

Name

Address

Telephone

Mobile

E-mail

Name

Address

Telephone

Mobile

E-mail

Name

Address

Telephone

Mobile

E-mail

Name

Address

Telephone

Mobile

E-mail

Name

Address

Telephone

Mobile

E-mail

ittle things mean alot

Name _____

Address _____

_____

_____

Telephone _____

Mobile _____

E-mail _____

Name _____

Address _____

_____

_____

Telephone _____

Mobile _____

E-mail _____

Name _____

Address _____

_____

_____

Telephone _____

Mobile _____

E-mail _____

Name _____

Address _____

_____

_____

Telephone _____

Mobile _____

E-mail _____

Name _____

Address _____

_____

_____

Telephone _____

Mobile _____

E-mail _____

Name _____

Address _____

_____

_____

Telephone _____

Mobile _____

E-mail _____

D

D

Name

Address

Telephone

Mobile

E-mail

Name

Address

Telephone

Mobile

E-mail

Name

Address

Telephone

Mobile

E-mail

Name

Address

Telephone

Mobile

E-mail

Name

Address

Telephone

Mobile

E-mail

Name

Address

Telephone

Mobile

E-mail

Name

Address

Telephone

Mobile

E-mail

Name

Address

Telephone

Mobile

E-mail

Name

Address

Telephone

Mobile

E-mail

Name

Address

Telephone

Mobile

E-mail

Name	Name
Address	Address
Telephone	Telephone
Mobile	Mobile
E-mail	E-mail
Name	Name
Address	Address
Telephone	Telephone
Mobile	Mobile
E-mail	E-mail
Name	Name
Address	Address
Telephone	Telephone
Mobile	Mobile
E-mail	E-mail

Name	Name
Address	Address
Telephone	Telephone
Mobile	Mobile
E-mail	E-mail
Name	Name
Address	Address
Telephone	Telephone
Mobile	Mobile
E-mail	E-mail

Name

Address

Telephone

Mobile

E-mail

chonk!

pop!

Name

Address

Telephone

Mobile

E-mail

Name

Address

Telephone

Mobile

E-mail

Name

Address

Telephone

Mobile

E-mail

Name

Address

Telephone

Mobile

E-mail

Name

Address

Telephone

Mobile

E-mail

life... is a puzzle

Name	Name
Address	Address
Telephone	Telephone
Mobile	Mobile
E-mail	E-mail

Name	Name
Address	Address
Telephone	Telephone
Mobile	Mobile
E-mail	E-mail

Name	Name
Address	Address
Telephone	Telephone
Mobile	Mobile
E-mail	E-mail

Name

Address

Telephone

Mobile

E-mail

Name

Address

Telephone

Mobile

E-mail

Name

Address

Telephone

Mobile

E-mail

Name

Address

Telephone

Mobile

E-mail

Name

Address

Telephone

Mobile

E-mail

Name

Address

Telephone

Mobile

E-mail

Name

Address

Telephone

Mobile

E-mail

Name

Address

Telephone

Mobile

E-mail

Name

Address

Telephone

Mobile

E-mail

Name

Address

Telephone

Mobile

E-mail

I think I'm getting in deep.....

Name	Name
Address	Address
Telephone	Telephone
Mobile	Mobile
E-mail	E-mail
Name	Name
Address	Address
Telephone	Telephone
Mobile	Mobile
E-mail	E-mail
Name	Name
Address	Address
Telephone	Telephone
Mobile	Mobile
E-mail	E-mail

Name

Address

Telephone

Mobile

E-mail

Name

Address

Telephone

Mobile

E-mail

Name

Address

Telephone

Mobile

E-mail

Name

Address

Telephone

Mobile

E-mail

Name

Address

Telephone

Mobile

E-mail

Name

Address

Telephone

Mobile

E-mail

Name

Address

Telephone

Mobile

E-mail

Name

Address

Telephone

Mobile

E-mail

Name

Address

Telephone

Mobile

E-mail

Name

Address

Telephone

Mobile

E-mail

G

Newtons no.1 best gardening tip...   Don't!

Name	Name
Address	Address
Telephone	Telephone
Mobile	Mobile
E-mail	E-mail
Name	Name
Address	Address
Telephone	Telephone
Mobile	Mobile
E-mail	E-mail
Name	Name
Address	Address
Telephone	Telephone
Mobile	Mobile
E-mail	E-mail

Name

Address

Telephone

Mobile

E-mail

Name

Address

Telephone

Mobile

E-mail

Name

Address

Telephone

Mobile

E-mail

Name

Address

Telephone

Mobile

E-mail

Name

Address

Telephone

Mobile

E-mail

Name

Address

Telephone

Mobile

E-mail

Name

Address

Telephone

Mobile

E-mail

Name

Address

Telephone

Mobile

E-mail

Name

Address

Telephone

Mobile

E-mail

Name

Address

Telephone

Mobile

E-mail

it's not the party you're at,
it's the list that you're on.

Name	Name
Address	Address
Telephone	Telephone
Mobile	Mobile
E-mail	E-mail
Name	Name
Address	Address
Telephone	Telephone
Mobile	Mobile
E-mail	E-mail
Name	Name
Address	Address
Telephone	Telephone
Mobile	Mobile
E-mail	E-mail

I

I

Name

Address

Telephone

Mobile

E-mail

Name

Address

Telephone

Mobile

E-mail

Name

Address

Telephone

Mobile

E-mail

Name

Address

Telephone

Mobile

E-mail

Name

Address

Telephone

Mobile

E-mail

Name	Name
Address	Address
Telephone	Telephone
Mobile	Mobile
E-mail	E-mail

Name	Name
Address	Address
Telephone	Telephone
Mobile	Mobile
E-mail	E-mail

Name	
Address	
Telephone	
Mobile	
E-mail	

always keep your eye on
the ball...

Name	Name
Address	Address
Telephone	Telephone
Mobile	Mobile
E-mail	E-mail

Name	Name
Address	Address
Telephone	Telephone
Mobile	Mobile
E-mail	E-mail

Name	Name
Address	Address
Telephone	Telephone
Mobile	Mobile
E-mail	E-mail

Name	Name
Address	Address
Telephone	Telephone
Mobile	Mobile
E-mail	E-mail
Name	Name
Address	Address
Telephone	Telephone
Mobile	Mobile
E-mail	E-mail
	Name
	Address
	Telephone
	Mobile
	E-mail

Name	Name
Address	Address
Telephone	Telephone
Mobile	Mobile
E-mail	E-mail
Name	Name
Address	Address
Telephone	Telephone
Mobile	Mobile
E-mail	E-mail
Name	
Address	
Telephone	
Mobile	
E-mail	

laughter is the
best medicine...

Name	Name
Address	Address
Telephone	Telephone
Mobile	Mobile
E-mail	E-mail
Name	Name
Address	Address
Telephone	Telephone
Mobile	Mobile
E-mail	E-mail
Name	Name
Address	Address
Telephone	Telephone
Mobile	Mobile
E-mail	E-mail

Name

Address

Telephone

Mobile

E-mail

Name

Address

Telephone

Mobile

E-mail

Name

Address

Telephone

Mobile

E-mail

Name

Address

Telephone

Mobile

E-mail

Name

Address

Telephone

Mobile

E-mail

Name

Address

Telephone

mobile

E-mail

Name

Address

Telephone

mobile

E-mail

Name

Address

Telephone

mobile

E-mail

Name

Address

Telephone

mobile

E-mail

Name

Address

Telephone

mobile

E-mail

don't be tempted to eat
anything bigger than

your head...

Name

Address

Telephone

Mobile

E-mail

Name

Address

Telephone

Mobile

E-mail

Name

Address

Telephone

Mobile

E-mail

Name

Address

Telephone

Mobile

E-mail

Name

Address

Telephone

Mobile

E-mail

Name

Address

Telephone

Mobile

E-mail

Name

Address

Telephone

Mobile

E-mail

Name

Address

Telephone

Mobile

E-mail

Name

Address

Telephone

Mobile

E-mail

Name

Address

Telephone

Mobile

E-mail

Name

Address

Telephone

Mobile

E-mail

Name

Address

Telephone

Mobile

E-mail

Name

Address

Telephone

Mobile

E-mail

Name

Address

Telephone

Mobile

E-mail

Name

Address

Telephone

Mobile

E-mail

Name

Address

Telephone

Mobile

E-mail

Name

Address

Telephone

Mobile

E-mail

luck is where you find it...

Name

Address

Telephone

Mobile

E-mail

Name

Address

Telephone

Mobile

E-mail

Name

Address

Telephone

Mobile

E-mail

Name

Address

Telephone

Mobile

E-mail

Name

Address

Telephone

Mobile

E-mail

hi!

now you say
something...

Name

Address

Telephone

Mobile

E-mail

Name

Address

Telephone

Mobile

E-mail

Name

Address

Telephone

Mobile

E-mail

Name

Address

Telephone

Mobile

E-mail

Name

Address

Telephone

Mobile

E-mail

Name

Address

Telephone

Mobile

E-mail

Name

Address

Telephone

Mobile

E-mail

Name

Address

Telephone

Mobile

E-mail

Name

Address

Telephone

Mobile

E-mail

Name

Address

Telephone

Mobile

E-mail

Name

Address

Telephone

Mobile

E-mail

Name	Name
Address	Address
Telephone	Telephone
Mobile	Mobile
E-mail	E-mail
Name	Name
Address	Address
Telephone	Telephone
Mobile	Mobile
E-mail	E-mail
Name	
Address	
Telephone	
Mobile	
E-mail	

Name	Name
Address	Address
Telephone	Telephone
Mobile	Mobile
E-mail	E-mail
Name	Name
Address	Address
Telephone	Telephone
Mobile	Mobile
E-mail	E-mail
Name	Name
Address	Address
Telephone	Telephone
Mobile	Mobile
E-mail	E-mail

Name

Address

Telephone

Mobile

E-mail

Name

Address

Telephone

Mobile

E-mail

Name

Address

Telephone

Mobile

E-mail

Name

Address

Telephone

Mobile

E-mail

Name

Address

Telephone

Mobile

E-mail

Name

Address

Telephone

Mobile

E-mail

Name

Address

Telephone

Mobile

E-mail

Name

Address

Telephone

Mobile

E-mail

Name

Address

Telephone

Mobile

E-mail

Name

Address

Telephone

Mobile

E-mail

the sky's the limit, they said.

Name	Name
Address	Address
Telephone	Telephone
Mobile	Mobile
E-mail	E-mail

Name	Name
Address	Address
Telephone	Telephone
Mobile	Mobile
E-mail	E-mail

Name	Name
Address	Address
Telephone	Telephone
Mobile	Mobile
E-mail	E-mail

P

Name

Address

Telephone

Mobile

E-mail

Name

Address

Telephone

Mobile

E-mail

Name

Address

Telephone

Mobile

E-mail

Name

Address

Telephone

Mobile

E-mail

Name

Address

Telephone

Mobile

E-mail

P

Name	Name
Address	Address
Telephone	Telephone
Mobile	Mobile
E-mail	E-mail

Name	Name
Address	Address
Telephone	Telephone
Mobile	Mobile
E-mail	E-mail

Name

Address

Telephone

Mobile

E-mail

P

be an exhibtionist –
show someone your love

Name	Name
Address	Address
Telephone	Telephone
Mobile	Mobile
E-mail	E-mail

Name	Name
Address	Address
Telephone	Telephone
Mobile	Mobile
E-mail	E-mail

Name	Name
Address	Address
Telephone	Telephone
Mobile	Mobile
E-mail	E-mail

Q

Name

Address

Telephone

Mobile

E-mail

Name

Address

Telephone

Mobile

E-mail

Name

Address

Telephone

Mobile

E-mail

Name

Address

Telephone

Mobile

E-mail

Name

Address

Telephone

Mobile

E-mail

Name

Address

Telephone

Mobile

E-mail

Name

Address

Telephone

Mobile

E-mail

Name

Address

Telephone

Mobile

E-mail

Name

Address

Telephone

Mobile

E-mail

Name

Address

Telephone

Mobile

E-mail

Q

Name	Name
Address	Address
Telephone	Telephone
Mobile	Mobile
E-mail	E-mail
Name	Name
Address	Address
Telephone	Telephone
Mobile	Mobile
E-mail	E-mail
Name	Name
Address	Address
Telephone	Telephone
Mobile	Mobile
E-mail	E-mail

R

Name

Address

Telephone

Mobile

E-mail

Name

Address

Telephone

Mobile

E-mail

Name

Address

Telephone

Mobile

E-mail

Name

Address

Telephone

Mobile

E-mail

Name

Address

Telephone

Mobile

E-mail

R

Name

Address

Telephone

Mobile

E-mail

Name

Address

Telephone

Mobile

E-mail

Name

Address

Telephone

Mobile

E-mail

Name

Address

Telephone

Mobile

E-mail

Name

Address

Telephone

Mobile

E-mail

Name

Address

Telephone

Mobile

E-mail

R

what's it all about?

Name	Name
Address	Address
Telephone	Telephone
Mobile	Mobile
E-mail	E-mail
Name	Name
Address	Address
Telephone	Telephone
Mobile	Mobile
E-mail	E-mail
Name	Name
Address	Address
Telephone	Telephone
Mobile	Mobile
E-mail	E-mail

S

Name

Address

Telephone

Mobile

E-mail

Name

Address

Telephone

Mobile

E-mail

Name

Address

Telephone

Mobile

E-mail

Name

Address

Telephone

Mobile

E-mail

Name

Address

Telephone

Mobile

E-mail

S

Name

Address

Telephone

Mobile

E-mail

Name

Address

Telephone

Mobile

E-mail

Name

Address

Telephone

Mobile

E-mail

Name

Address

Telephone

Mobile

E-mail

Name

Address

Telephone

Mobile

E-mail

S

friendship counts

Name	Name
Address	Address
Telephone	Telephone
Mobile	Mobile
E-mail	E-mail
Name	Name
Address	Address
Telephone	Telephone
Mobile	Mobile
E-mail	E-mail
Name	Name
Address	Address
Telephone	Telephone
Mobile	Mobile
E-mail	E-mail

T

Name

Address

Telephone

Mobile

E-mail

Name

Address

Telephone

Mobile

E-mail

Name

Address

Telephone

Mobile

E-mail

Name

Address

Telephone

Mobile

E-mail

Name

Address

Telephone

Mobile

E-mail

T

Name

Address

Telephone

Mobile

E-mail

Name

Address

Telephone

Mobile

E-mail

Name

Address

Telephone

Mobile

E-mail

Name

Address

Telephone

Mobile

E-mail

Name

Address

Telephone

Mobile

E-mail

Name

Address

Telephone

Mobile

E-mail

T

Always be number one bring your own box...

Name	Name
Address	Address
Telephone	Telephone
Mobile	Mobile
E-mail	E-mail

Name	Name
Address	Address
Telephone	Telephone
Mobile	Mobile
E-mail	E-mail

Name	Name
Address	Address
Telephone	Telephone
Mobile	Mobile
E-mail	E-mail

UV

Name

Address

Telephone

Mobile

E-mail

Name

Address

Telephone

Mobile

E-mail

Name

Address

Telephone

Mobile

E-mail

Name

Address

Telephone

Mobile

E-mail

Name

Address

Telephone

Mobile

E-mail

UV

Name

Address

Telephone

Mobile

E-mail

Name

Address

Telephone

Mobile

E-mail

Name

Address

Telephone

Mobile

E-mail

Name

Address

Telephone

Mobile

E-mail

Name

Address

Telephone

Mobile

E-mail

UV

take time
to think..

Name	Name
Address	Address
Telephone	Telephone
Mobile	Mobile
E-mail	E-mail
Name	Name
Address	Address
Telephone	Telephone
Mobile	Mobile
E-mail	E-mail
Name	Name
Address	Address
Telephone	Telephone
Mobile	Mobile
E-mail	E-mail

W

Name

Address

Telephone

Mobile

E-mail

Name

Address

Telephone

Mobile

E-mail

Name

Address

Telephone

Mobile

E-mail

Name

Address

Telephone

Mobile

E-mail

Name

Address

Telephone

Mobile

E-mail

Name

Address

Telephone

Mobile

E-mail

Name

Address

Telephone

Mobile

E-mail

Name

Address

Telephone

Mobile

E-mail

Name

Address

Telephone

Mobile

E-mail

Name

Address

Telephone

Mobile

E-mail

W

keep calm......at all times

Name	Name
Address	Address
Telephone	Telephone
Mobile	Mobile
E-mail	E-mail

Name	Name
Address	Address
Telephone	Telephone
Mobile	Mobile
E-mail	E-mail

Name	Name
Address	Address
Telephone	Telephone
Mobile	Mobile
E-mail	E-mail

xy

Name

Address

Telephone

Mobile

E-mail

Name

Address

Telephone

Mobile

E-mail

Name

Address

Telephone

Mobile

E-mail

Name

Address

Telephone

Mobile

E-mail

Name

Address

Telephone

Mobile

E-mail

xy

Name

Address

Telephone

Mobile

E-mail

Name

Address

Telephone

Mobile

E-mail

Name

Address

Telephone

Mobile

E-mail

Name

Address

Telephone

Mobile

E-mail

Name

Address

Telephone

Mobile

E-mail

xy

Name

Address

Telephone

Mobile

E-mail

Name

Address

Telephone

Mobile

E-mail

Name

Address

Telephone

Mobile

E-mail

Name

Address

Telephone

Mobile

E-mail

Name

Address

Telephone

Mobile

E-mail

Name

Address

Telephone

Mobile

E-mail

happy birthday!
Important note! Birthda
B'DAY reminder
DON'T FORGET!
Don't Forget
ha! I remembered.

Birthdays, events and Anniversaries

January

1	2	3	4
5	6	7	8
9	10	11	12
13	14	15	16

January

17	18	19	20
21	22	23	24
25	26	27	28
29	30	31	

February

1	2	3	4
5	6	7	8
9	10	11	12
13	14	15	16

February

17	18	19	20
21	22	23	24
25	26	27	28
29			

march

1	2	3	4
5	6	7	8
9	10	11	12
13	14	15	16

march

17	18	19	20
21	22	23	24
25	26	27	28
29	30	31	

April

1	2	3	4
5	6	7	8
9	10	11	12
13	14	15	16

April

17	18	19	20
21	22	23	24
25	26	27	28
29	30		

May

1	2	3	4
5	6	7	8
9	10	11	12
13	14	15	16

may

17	18	19	20
21	22	23	24
25	26	27	28
29	30	31	

June

1	2	3	4
5	6	7	8
9	10	11	12
13	14	15	16

June

17	18	19	20
21	22	23	24
25	26	27	28
29	30		

July

1	2	3	4
5	6	7	8
9	10	11	12
13	14	15	16

July

17	18	19	20
21	22	23	24
25	26	27	28
29	30	31	

August

1	2	3	4
5	6	7	8
9	10	11	12
13	14	15	16

August

17	18	19	20
21	22	23	24
25	26	27	28
29	30	31	

September

1	2	3	4
5	6	7	8
9	10	11	12
13	14	15	16

September

17	18	19	20
21	22	23	24
25	26	27	28
29	30		

October

1	2	3	4
5	6	7	8
9	10	11	12
13	14	15	16

October

17	18	19	20
21	22	23	24
25	26	27	28
29	30	31	

November

1	2	3	4
5	6	7	8
9	10	11	12
13	14	15	16

November

17	18	19	20
21	22	23	24
25	26	27	28
29	30		

December

1	2	3	4
5	6	7	8
9	10	11	12
13	14	15	16

December

17	18	19	20
21	22	23	24
25	26	27	28
29	30	31	

Christmas Card List

Name	Year	Sent	Received

Name	Year	Sent	Received

Christmas Card List

Name	Year	Sent	Received

Name	Year	Sent	Received

Christmas Card List

Name	Year	Sent	Received

Name	Year	Sent	Received

Christmas Card List

Name	Year	Sent	Received

Name	Year	Sent	Received

Christmas Card List

Name	Year	Sent	Received

Name	Year	Sent	Received

Christmas Card List

Name	Year	Sent	Received

clear your mind –
make a list...

Gifts and Ideas List

Name	Occasion	Date

Name	Occasion	Date

Name	Occasion	Date

Name	Occasion	Date

Name	Occasion	Date

Name	Occasion	Date

Name	Occasion	Date

Name	Occasion	Date

Name	Occasion	Date

Name	Occasion	Date
....	....	....
....	....	....
....	....	....
....	....	....
....	....	....
....	....	....
....	....	....
....	....	....
....	....	....
....	....	....
....	....	....
....	....	....
....	....	....
....	....	....
....	....	....
....	....	....
....	....	....
....	....	....
....	....	....
....	....	....
....	....	....

Name	Occasion	Date

Name	Occasion	Date

Name	Occasion	Date

Name	Occasion	Date

Name	Occasion	Date

Name	Occasion	Date

Name	Occasion	Date

Name	Occasion	Date

Name	Occasion	Date